HOME

That's Gross!
A Look at Science

Julie Murray

VISIT US AT
www.abdopublishing.com

Published by ABDO Publishing Company, 8000 West 78th Street, Edina, Minnesota 55439.

Coordinating Series Editor: Rochelle Baltzer
Editor: Sarah Tieck
Contributing Editor: Marcia Zappa
Graphic Design: Deborah Coldiron
Cover Photograph: *AnimalsAnimals-Earth Scenes:* OSF/Science Pictures Limited; *iStockPhoto:* Michal Rozanski; *Photos.com:* Jupiter Images.
Interior Photographs/Illustrations: *AnimalsAnimals-Earth Scenes*: OSF/London Scientific Films (p. 7); *AP Photo:* Miranda Meyer/The Gazette (p. 27); *Getty Images:* Bryan Mullenix (p. 27); *iStockPhoto:* Artemenko Aleksey (p. 25), Felipe Bello (p. 19), Mike Bentley (p. 21), Dan Brandenburg (p. 15), Jani Bryson (pp. 23, 24), Adrian Costea (p. 15) Joe Daniel (p. 11), Marc Dietrich (p. 13), Wendell Franks (p. 5), Andrea Gingerich (p. 21), Eileen Hart (p. 17), David Hernandez (pp. 29, 30), Hubert Inabinet (p. 19), iStockPhoto (pp. 21, 29), Bonnie Jacobs (p. 10), Mike Jones (p. 19), Jim Jurica (p. 15), Bela Tibor Kozma (p. 7), Cat London (p. 28), Richard Martyniak (p. 9), Liza McCorkle (p. 7), Vasko Miokovic (p. 23), Slobo Mitic (pp. 23, 30), Oktay Ortakcfoglu (p. 29), Brian Pamphilon (p. 20), Elizabeth Peardon (p. 22), Paul Rosado (p. 11), Martti Salmela (p. 21), Alice Scully (p. 23), Victor Zastol Skiy (p. 5), Mike Sonnenberg (pp. 13, 18, 27); *Peter Arnold, Inc.:* Matt Meadows (p. 9), Darlyne A. Murawski (p. 7), Ed Reschke (p. 17), David Scharf (p. 17); *Photos.com:* Jupiter Images (pp. 5, 9, 12, 13, 17).

Library of Congress Cataloging-in-Publication Data

Murray, Julie, 1969-
  Home / Julie Murray.
     p. cm. -- (That's gross! A look at science)
  ISBN 978-1-60453-555-6
  1. Microbial ecology--Juvenile literature. 2. Household ecology--Juvenile literature. 3. Housing and health--Juvenile literature. I. Title.
  QR57.M87 2009
  577.5'54--dc22
                          2008037172

Contents

Exploring Home

Your home is amazing! It provides housing. It offers safety. And, it is a place for families to live and love. Look a little closer. You'll see that behind all that cool stuff is a lot of yuck. Some of it is natural. Some of it is unhealthy. Let's explore!

Your kitchen, bathroom, and bedroom may not seem gross. But, icky things are likely hiding beneath the surface.

Creepy Crawlies

There are very small bugs called dust mites all over your home! These see-through, white spiders feed on pieces of dead human skin. They also like the wetness of human sweat.

Most dust mites live about one to three months. In that time, they create a lot of poop and other waste. Their poop causes **allergy** (A-luhr-jee) problems. This is a bigger problem for people with **asthma** (AZ-muh).

No way!
One female dust mite can lay up to 80 eggs in her life! Yuck!

A used mattress can have 10,000 to 10 million dust mites in it!

Dust mites are so small, you can only see them with a magnifying glass. They hide in pillows, couches, and rugs.

Another type of bug in some homes is a bedbug. Bedbugs hide in beds and beneath floors. They come out and bite people while they are sleeping.

Every few days, bedbugs must eat. They feed on human blood. They have special beaks to help them bite people and suck out blood.

Bedbugs are found in clean and dirty places. They get into homes by crawling or traveling on clothes and furniture. It is hard to get rid of bedbugs!

Sleep tight . . .
People with bedbugs notice small, itchy bite marks on their legs.

Bedbugs leave droppings and other waste. ick!

9

Stinky, Steamy Toilet

Many years ago, houses didn't have plumbing (PLUH-mihng). So, people used outhouses. These didn't have flushing toilets. Poop and pee piled up in a big hole. And, many outhouses didn't have toilet paper. Instead, people used newspaper or paper from old books.

On hot summer days, flies buzzed in stinky outhouses. But, many people thought this was better than using the grass as a toilet!

Guess what?

Before toilets, some people would poop and pee in small pots in their bedrooms. These were called chamber pots. After the pots were used, people had to empty them.

Old-fashioned outhouses were made of wood. Many had a moon carved into the door. Today's outhouses are called portable toilets. These are made of plastic and are often found at outdoor events.

Open Wide

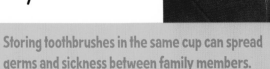

All kinds of bacteria (bak-TIHR-ee-uh) and germs (JUHRMS) live on your toothbrush. Some of them come from the toilet!

Scientists say the toilet can spray more than four feet (1.2 m) every time it is flushed. This leaves very small amounts of poop and pee on stuff in the bathroom. That includes your toothbrush. Usually, it is not enough to make you sick. But, it is still yucky!

Storing toothbrushes in the same cup can spread germs and sickness between family members.

Some researchers say toilet water is cleaner than ice in drinks at restaurants!

You don't say!

The spray from a toilet flush is called "the aerosol effect." This is because it sprays like the aerosol cans that some hair and cleaning sprays come in.

All Stopped Up

Used water flows out of your home through pipes. But sometimes, pipes don't work properly.

Plumbing problems are usually caused by greasy, hairy **clogs** (KLAHGS). Clogs fill up pipes. This causes everything that flows through to get caught. Dirty water may flood the sink or the bathtub. The toilet might even overflow! To get things moving, the clog must be broken up and cleared out.

Leftover food in sinks can cause clogs (*above*). Clogs also happen when hair collects in bathtub drains (*below*).

Plumbers use special tools, such as plungers, to get clogs moving.

15

How About Some Dinner?

The kitchen might look clean, but it is one of the grossest spots in the house. Scientists found that kitchen sinks have high levels of **germs** and **bacteria**. Many are dirtier than a **flushed** toilet!

Sponges are even yuckier than sinks. Germs love to grow in warm, wet spaces. So even if a sponge looks clean, it might be full of bacteria. Wiping off a counter with a sponge could make the counter even dirtier!

16

No worries!
Soap and water can kill many germs. Use a clean, soapy rag to wash door handles, the refrigerator, and the telephone.

Bacteria are tiny. A person cannot see them without a special tool called a microscope.

If you help make dinner, be sure to wash your hands after touching raw meat. **Bacteria** such as E. coli and salmonella can live in the bloody flesh and fat. These make people very sick.

Cooking meat on the grill or in the oven helps kill bacteria. But, the meat must reach a certain **temperature** (TEHM-puhr-chur) before all the bacteria die. This makes the meat safe to eat.

When preparing meat, wash all surfaces that raw meat has touched. After meat is cooked, place it on a clean surface.

A thermometer measures the temperature of meat. You can also cut open a piece of meat to see if it is cooked enough.

19

Mount Washmore

What's in that pile of stinky laundry? When wet towels, sweaty gym shirts, and used underwear sit piled together, it is likely there's **mildew**. As it grows, mildew eats away at towels and clothes. This creates a gross odor and can cause **allergy** problems.

It doesn't take long for mildew to get out of control. It can grow on clothes (*right*), in books, and even on buildings (*below*)!

21

Finders Keepers?

What's hiding in your refrigerator? Ever find bread covered in **mold**? How about rotting leftovers from last month? Ever touch a gooey, dripping piece of fruit that has gone soft? Refrigerators are full of gross discoveries!

Mold can grow on both the outside and inside of foods.

Clean up your act

Refrigerators should be regularly washed and cleaned out. This keeps them from getting smelly and gross. It also helps prevent the growth of mold.

23

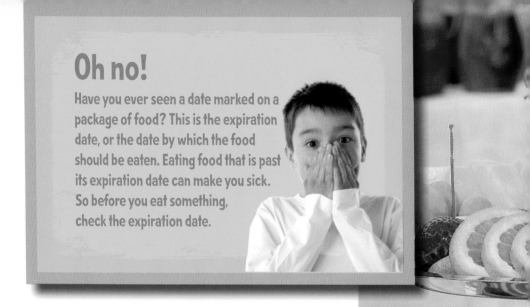

Certain foods should stay refrigerated. If they are left out too long, unsafe bacteria begin to grow. Sometimes this makes the food look gross or smell sour. It might still taste fine. But, eating unsafe food can cause sicknesses such as upset stomach, fever, and diarrhea (deye-uh-REE-uh)!

Two hours is the limit for food to be outside the refrigerator. After that, it might become unsafe to eat.

All-You-Can-Eat Buffet

Termites look kind of like ants. They feed on wood. Termites sometimes get inside homes, where they can cause a lot of harm! In the forest, termites eat dead trees. This helps keep forests healthy. Those millions of tiny bugs can eat wood until it is gone!

These nasty critters live in large groups that can include millions of bugs.

Can you believe it?

The Yanomami who live in the Amazon eat termites! They cook them inside of banana leaves.

Termites can destroy papers and books, too.

27

That WAS Gross!

Between dust mites, stinky laundry, and **moldy** food, some very yucky things are in your home!

Now that you know about all the grossness, take a closer look. Many gross things are just a part of life and no big deal. Others can be prevented. Do what you can to live in a healthy way!

Did you know that about one in three people don't wash their hands after using the bathroom? Yuck! Hand washing is important. Be sure to use soap and warm water.

Sneezing and stuffy noses can be a sign of allergies or sickness. Dusting and cleaning surfaces helps prevent this.

Vacuuming is one way to keep your space tidy. This helps make your home a healthy place.

Eeeeww! What is THAT?

Answer on page 32.

30

Important Words

allergy a condition in which coughing, sneezing, or a rash develops when a person comes in contact with a certain thing.

asthma a condition that causes wheezing and coughing and makes it hard to breathe.

bacteria tiny one-celled organisms that can only be seen through a microscope. Some are germs.

clog a blockage.

diarrhea a condition in which a person has loose bowel movements, or poop, that happen too often.

flush to wash out with a sudden flow of water.

germs harmful organisms that can make people sick.

mildew a living thing called a fungus that commonly grows on plants, fabric, or paper.

mold a living thing called a fungus that commonly grows on food.

plumbing the pipes and other parts of a building's water system.

temperature the measured level of hot or cold.

Web Sites

To learn more about gross stuff, visit ABDO Publishing Company online. Web sites about gross stuff are featured on our Book Links page. These links are routinely monitored and updated to provide the most current information available.

www.abdopublishing.com

Index

"Eeeeww! What is THAT?" answer: mold growing on a tomato.